You've Been Called!

By: Mary Murray

Mission Ministries

Inspiring Life and Hope to Women
Mary Murray 314-769-7129
www.missionm.org   mary@missionm.org

Thank you!

I want to dedicate this Epistle of Edification to all the women that have helped me along the way. All of the words of correction and discipline you gave from love; are one of the greatest gifts God has given me. You have supported me in every way.

Your grace and mercy on my life have given me the courage to keep moving forward. Let me add…you never knew that many times it hurt and sometimes I cried, but I always felt loved and inspired, because of you.

A special thank you to Janice Mc. Bride; my wee Scottish mum who kept me in the Word and wouldn't let me get away with, "But" you don't understand. I love you Janice.

Gary, thank you so much for your unconditional love and occasional pushes; I love you very much. God knew just who I needed in to be my mate in this life.

Table of Contents

Acknowledgement	3
Introduction	5
Part One You've been called	9
Part Two Count the Cost	27
Part Three Go for It	33
About the Author	53

Introduction

The fact that we as Christians have been called is a given. The fact that we do not respond to that call is a state many of us stay in due to lack of understanding.

I have written this exhortation to encourage and motivate you to step up to the call God has placed on your life: For you to be all He has already built in you to be. However, for one reason or other, you have been held back.

It is a very scary thing to stand up in front of people and speak, lecture, teach or preach. I remember the first time God called on me to minister and I thought, I just cannot, and you know what, I could not, nor can you, but He can and will through you.

As you read these pages, you will see yourself and move past the lack of understanding. You will learn to count the cost, and finally you will see yourself ministering as God gives you open doors to your family, friends and neighbors.

My prayer for you is that as you read this handbook, you will say Yes, Lord, Yes!

Reference from NIV unless otherwise noted by name.
This booklet is not to be reproduced or copied without written consent from Mary Murray.
Thank you Pam Row, Ken Puckett and Chris Sheeley

Part 1

You've Been Called!

I remember when I was a little girl living in cold water flat with my mom and little sister; by now by brothers had moved out or joined the Army. We were poor and my mom worked very hard to support us. She did a great job. One winter it was so cold that she took the chairs from our kitchen table and burned them in the pot-bellied stove to get us warm. That year we went from having a table with a leaf in it and six chairs to a table with no leaf and three chairs, but we were warm.

Looking back on my childhood I now believe this was the first time God was calling me, but at that tender age, I did not know it. Often times my mother would come home from work with migraine headaches and ask me to pray for her. We did not go to church as there was none near us and we did not have a car. My mom grew up in church and had a relationship with Jesus. I know because she would always pray aloud, and ask Jesus to help her. Clearly He did, because we survived those years. Anyway, I would put my hand on her head and pray and God would heal her. I had no idea what I was doing, but my mom knew the power of prayer and laying on of hands, and I had a great love for this wonderful man named Jesus.

One day I remember vividly drawing three crosses on our living room wall; putting the larger one in the middle with rays of light coming from it. I must have been very young, because my dad still lived there and my actions made him angry. He was a paperhanger and he had just finished papering the living room. He yelled at me in one of his drunken stupors and I can remember him saying, "How do I know that stuff is real?" I remember clearly telling him that I knew Jesus was real.

There were many other times, as I look back over my life, that I heard God call me through other people and or situations. I bet if you will do the same, you too will remember times He was calling your name and instructing you.

The key is learning to listen. God calls everyone; we all have a call on our lives. The question is what is holding you back from fulfilling that call? My prayer for you is when you are finished reading this epistle of encouragement, God's zeal will be renewed, and His fire will be roaring within you so that you will fulfill the works He called you too.

Romans 8:28-31
We know that in all things God works for the good of those who love him, who have been called according to His purpose. For those God foreknew he also predestined to be conformed to the likeness of his Son, that he might be the firstborn among many brothers. And those he predestined, he also called; those he called, he also justified; those he justified, he also glorified.

I love these verses and want to expound on them a little. For instance, the word justified is best understood when you realize the moment you asked God for forgiveness, He not only forgave you, but also threw your sins as far as the east is from the west. I loved what my pastor said when I was a baby Christian.

He said, "You have been justified, just as if you hadn't done it". I liked that, it was simple and easy to remember. We will look at the word glorified later, but let us look at two other things right now.

First, you know that God called you and that He has a purpose for your life. You were born with a special talent, you are unique, and there is only one person like you. There are people God has put in your life that no one can minister to but you. You are His child and you belong to Him.

Secondly, the call of ministry God has on your life was predestined. What does that mean?

2 Timothy 1:9
God has saved us and called us to a holy life-not because of anything we have done but because of his own purpose and grace. This grace was given us in Christ Jesus before the beginning of time,

While reading this powerful scripture, let it go deep into your soul to build you up spiritually. He knew you in the womb and knew how you would respond to His voice, to His knock. That does not mean you will not kick against the pricks as Saul/Paul; [as I like to call him], did to Jesus when the Lord was calling Saul.

Acts 26:14
Saul, Saul, why do you persecute me? It is hard for you to kick against the goads.' It is hard for thee to kick against the ox-goads, as the unbroken bullock does to his own hurt, instead of quietly submitting, as he must do at last, to go the way and the pace his master chooses he should go.

(From The Pulpit Commentary, Electronic Database. Copyright (c) 2001 by Biblesoft)

Why do we struggle so hard within ourselves? Once we have felt the touch of God, we cannot go back. We know that in the end we will follow Jesus! After all, we were born to glorify Him. The word glorify means to magnify God through praising His name and honoring Him. Jesus glorified His father through His perfect obedience and His sacrificial death on our behalf. How can we then, glorify God?

John 17:1-5
After Jesus said this, he looked toward heaven and prayed: "Father, the time has come. Glorify your Son, that your Son may glorify you. For you granted him authority over all people that he might give eternal life to all those you have given him. Now this is eternal life: that they may know you, the only true God, and Jesus Christ, whom you have sent. I have brought you glory on earth by completing the work you gave me to do. Now, Father, glorify me in your presence with the glory I had with you before the world began.

When you perform signs and wonders for the Lord, He is glorified and so are you. Not in the sense of, "Oh isn't she great, look what she did", no, but instead, look what God did through her. When these things happen, you are glorifying the Lord.

If you are not walking in that call, it is because you have laid it down. You are kicking against the pricks, or maybe, the time has not come for you until now. No matter, which it is, now is the time. How do I know that? You are reading this exhortation. We have very little time left to do God's bidding in the world. Things are rapidly changing and you do not want to miss out, nor do you want to leave anyone behind.

You have been called...that's a given...now let us examine why you are not walking to the fullness of that call. We know that it is either a physical reason or a spiritual one.

The physical or natural reasons that hold us back can sometimes be so obvious that we totally miss them.

How about money or the lack of? It is always a good thing to blame our problems on. For instance, I cannot go on the mission trip, I have no money. I cannot make it to church, the Bible study, the prayer meeting, the women's meeting or whatever other gathering you may need to be at in order to grow in your spiritual understanding. Some of you may say you cannot afford to buy the study materials. On the other hand, maybe you think your clothes are not good enough for the event. Alternatively, you may not have enough gas to get there. Can you see where I am going with this? However, I find it very odd that we, [and I think it is safe to say we here] quite often have money for the things we really want to do.

It is important to see things the way God intends you to. He has given us a set of principles to live by regarding money. Tithe the first fruits of your labors to your church, spend wisely, which means to be careful with what He gives you and you will see your money stretch. I know this first hand. I have been in positions before where I did not know how my bills were going to be paid, but they always were. God is faithful! He even challenges us to test Him in this principle in the book of Malachi. In fact, this is the only place in the whole Bible that we are given permission to test Him.

There are so many scriptures telling us that our heavenly Father will take care of us. He loves us. Just look how He instructed the Israelites while they were in the desert when it came to the manna from heaven. It was free, but they did have to do something for it...they had to gather it. Yet, they did not have to work on Sundays or do any overtime.

Exodus 16:17-19
The Israelites did as they were told; some gathered much, some little. And when they measured it by the omer, he who gathered much did not have too much, and he who gathered little did not have too little. Each one gathered as much as he needed.

Exodus 16:22-26
On the sixth day, they gathered twice as much--two omers for each person--and the leaders of the community came and reported this to Moses. He said to them, "This is what the LORD commanded: 'Tomorrow is to be a day of rest, a holy Sabbath to the LORD. So bake what you want to bake and boil what you want to boil. Save whatever is left and keep it until morning.'" So they saved it until morning, as Moses commanded, and it did not stink or get maggots in it. "Eat it today," Moses said, "because today is a Sabbath to the LORD. You will not find any of it on the ground today. Sabbath-rest... Six days you are to gather it, but on the seventh day, the Sabbath, there will not be any."

Some of us may have a problem with greed, which is another money issue. I understand that completely because I grew up poor. In fact, it is not so long ago that I came to a place in my life that I could actually get rid of things that no longer fit or that I no longer had need of because of that phrase, "I may need them someday." Everyone has those thoughts at one time or another, especially if you grew up poor. Well, here is how God feels about greed, and or amassing things. Before we look at these scriptures, let me say how important it is to keep a healthy balance when we study. We need to use wisdom as we read these scriptures and understand that the implication here is how we regard things. <u>I learned a long time ago that God does not care how much we have. What He cares about is what has us.</u>

Proverbs 21:17
He who loves pleasure will become poor; whoever loves wine and oil will never be rich.

Proverbs 21:20
In the house of the wise are stores of choice food and oil, but a foolish man devours all he has.

Numbers 11:1
The People whined and complained that they had no meat... they wanted meat.

Numbers 11:31-35
Now a wind went out from the LORD and drove quail in from the sea. It brought them down all around the camp to about three feet above the ground, as far as a day's walk in any direction. All that day and night and all the next day the people

went out and gathered quail. No one gathered less than ten homers. Then they spread them out all around the camp. But while the meat was still between their teeth and before it could be consumed, the anger of the LORD burned against the people, and he struck them with a severe plague. Therefore the place was named Kibroth Hattaavah, because there they buried the people who had craved other food.

You see, our God supplies all our needs, not necessarily all our wants. Yet when we are in His will, He gives us our wants too because our focus isn't on "me." Let me repeat this principle one more time. <u>God does not care about what you have, but what has you and what is most important to your hearts.</u>

Matthew 6:23
"No one can serve two masters. Either he will hate the one and love the other, or he will be devoted to the one and despise the other. You cannot serve both God and Money.

You can become bitter when you see what your worldly friends have and feel like you should have them too. To obtain what you think they have, you decide to work overtime on Wednesday nights and/or on Sundays. Maybe you will keep your tithe this week. After all, God does not need it, and you could sure use it. I really do know this first hand. I have been jealous of other people's possessions.

Matthew 6:25-35
"Therefore I tell you, do not worry about your life, what you will eat or drink; or about your body, what you will wear. Is not life more important than food,

and the body more important than clothes? Look at the birds of the air; they do not sow or reap or store away in barns, and yet your heavenly Father feeds them. Are you not much more valuable than they? Who of you by worrying can add a single hour to his life? And why do you worry about clothes? See how the lilies of the field grow. They do not labor or spin. Yet I tell you that not even Solomon in all his splendor was dressed like one of these. If that is how God clothes the grass of the field, which is here today and tomorrow is thrown into the fire, will he not much more clothe you, O you of little faith? So do not worry, saying, 'What shall we eat?' or 'What shall we drink?' or 'What shall we wear?' For the pagans run after all these things, and your heavenly Father knows that you need them. But seek first his kingdom and his righteousness, and all these things will be given to you as well. Therefore do not worry about tomorrow, for tomorrow will worry about itself. Each day has enough trouble of its own."

God has a wonderful balance, as you will see when you read the following scripture.

1 Timothy 6:5-10
But godliness with contentment is great gain. For we brought nothing into the world, and we can take nothing out of it. But if we have food and clothing, we will be content with that. People who want to get rich fall into temptation and a trap and into many foolish and harmful desires that plunge men into ruin and destruction. For the love of money is a root of all kinds of evil. Some people, eager for money, have wandered from the faith and pierced themselves with many sorrows.

Perhaps the reason you are not ministering is that your husband will not let you. He is very jealous of your time; he gets angry when you are gone, or he is not a Christian. These are valid reasons; however, if you are willing to be honest with yourself and the Lord, you may learn some things that when faced, God will reveal some truths to you that will strengthen and free you. After all, you are reading this in private and God wants to talk to you.

Here are a few good questions to ask yourself. Have you really prayed about this situation? Have you really prayed for him? Have you talked to him honestly about this? On the other hand, have you complained so much about all the time *"it"* takes or have you put the ministry in front of him in such a way that he feels insecure and or rejected? Alternatively, is he really the reason? How much time are you on the phone when your husband is home and he would like your company, but you are "doing God's work"? I have been this woman and when it was pointed out to me, I asked God what to do. I sat down with my husband and told him my heart's desire and then I asked for his help. Wow, what a revelation that brought! Not only did he support me, he became my biggest encourager.

I want to expound on this particular scripture as it came up in a conversation recently and I want to share it with you. I will paraphrase it, but at the same time, I want to encourage you to read the text yourself.

1 Samuel 25:1-41 [Paraphrased] When Samuel died, David moved down into Paran in Carmel. A very wealthy man named Nabal lived there with his wife, Abigail. It was shearing time and he had a thousand goats and three thousand sheep, which he was shearing in Carmel. His wife was an intelligent and beautiful woman, but her husband was surly and mean in his dealings.

While David was in the desert, he heard that Nabal was shearing sheep. Therefore, he sent ten young men and said to them, **"Go greet him in my name, saying, and 'Long life to you! Good health to you and your household! And good health to all that is yours! Now I hear that it is sheep-shearing time. When your shepherds were with us, we did not mistreat them, and nothing of theirs was missing. Ask your servants and they will tell you. Therefore, be favorable toward my young men, since we come at a festive time. Please give your servants and your son David whatever you can find for them."**

David's men arrived, and gave Nabil this message then waited. Nabil answered David's servants, **"Who is this David? Who is this son of Jesse? Many servants are breaking away from their masters these days. Why should I take my bread and water, and the meat I have slaughtered for my shearers, and give it to men coming from who knows where?"**

David's men did not say he was the son of Jesse…this response shows the character of the man Nabil. He indeed knew who David was! This was a great insult.

David's men turned around and went back. When they arrived, they reported every word. David said to his men, **"Put on your swords!"** Therefore, they put on their swords, and David put on his. About four hundred men went up with David, while two hundred stayed with the supplies.

One of the servants told Nabil's wife Abigail everything that had happened and that **"David and his men were very good to them. They did not mistreat us, and the whole time we were out in the fields near them, nothing was missing. Night and day they were a wall around us all the time we were herding our sheep near them. Think it over and see what you can do, because disaster is hanging over our master and his whole household. He is such a wicked man that no one can talk to him."**

1 Samuel 25:18-23
Abigail lost no time. She took two hundred loaves of bread, two skins of wine, five dressed sheep, five seas of roasted grain, a hundred cakes of raisins and two hundred cakes of pressed figs, and loaded them on donkeys. Then she told her servants, "Go on ahead; I'll follow you." But she did not tell her husband Nabil. As she came riding her donkey into a mountain ravine, there were David and his men descending toward her, and she met them. David had just said, "It's been useless-all my watching over this fellow's property in the desert so that nothing of his was missing. He has paid me back evil for good. May God deal with David, be it ever so severely, if by morning I leave alive one male of all who belong to him!"

I read all my commentaries and there was not one explanation for why Abigail did not tell her husband. I can only assess from that, that there are occasions when a God-fearing woman must follow what she knows is right. I am not advocating that we women ignore our husband's wishes, but there are times when we must follow what is right no matter what. Peter said in the book of Acts, that he himself **"must obey God rather than man."**

1 Samuel 25:23-25
When Abigail saw David, she quickly got off her donkey and bowed down before David with her face to the ground. She fell at his feet and said: "My lord, let the blame be on me alone. Please let your servant speak to you; hear what your servant has to say. May my lord pay no attention to that wicked man Nabil. He is just like his name-his name is Fool, and folly goes with him. But as for me, your servant, I did not see the men my master sent.

She gave him the gift of food and asked for forgiveness. David told, Abigail, **"Praise be to the LORD, the God of Israel, who has sent you today to meet me, may you be blessed for your good judgment and for keeping me from bloodshed this day and from avenging myself with my own hands."**

When you as a woman are in a position to make things happen, it is vital that you use good judgment. You have to weigh the problem, pray over your heart and mind's decisions and see what the word of God says about it. If it is unclear, you must measure to the very best of your ability, discern, and separate good and evil in the situation, never, never choosing out of your wants for the end solutions.

When Abigail went back home, Nabal was in the house holding a banquet like that of a king. He was in high spirits and very drunk. Therefore, she told him nothing until daybreak. As you can see; this indeed is a very wise woman. She knew when to speak and more importantly, when not to.

Then in the morning, when Nabal was sober, his wife told him all these things, and his heart failed him and he became like a stone. She waited to talk to him. TIMING IS EVERYTHING!

Most of the commentaries said his heart failed him because of what he almost brought on himself and his household, one, however, said he was angry because his wife gave so much away. We know he was a greedy man from the words he spoke to his servants.

1 Samuel 25:38-40
About ten days later, the LORD struck Nabal and he died. When David heard that Nabal was dead, he said, "Praise be to the LORD, who has upheld my cause against Nabal for treating me with contempt. He has kept his servant from doing wrong and has brought Nabil's wrongdoing down on his own head."

Another reason we do not minister are the excuses that, "I'm not smart enough" or "I'm not good enough" or "I'm not spiritual enough. "

Isaiah 5:21
Woe to those who are wise in their own eyes and clever in their own sight.

1 Corinthians 1:18-19
For the message of the cross is foolishness to those who are perishing, but to us who are being saved it is the power of God. For it is written: "I

will destroy the wisdom of the wise; the intelligence of the intelligent I will frustrate."

1 Corinthians 3:16-21
Don't you know that you yourselves are God's temple and that God's Spirit lives in you? If anyone destroys God's temple, God will destroy him; for God's temple is sacred, and you are that temple. Do not deceive yourselves. If any one of you thinks he is wise by the standards of this age, he should become a "fool" so that he may become wise. For the wisdom of this world is foolishness in God's sight. As it is written: "He catches the wise in their craftiness"; and again, "The Lord knows that the thoughts of the wise are futile."

Mark 4:10-11
When he was alone, the Twelve and the others around him asked him about the parables. Jesus told them, "The secret of the kingdom of God has been given to you. But to those on the outside everything is said in parables

Matthew 13:11-12
Jesus replied, "The knowledge of the secrets of the kingdom of heaven has been given to you, but not to them. Whoever has will be given more, and he will have abundance. Whoever does not have, even what he has will be taken from him.

There are many things that keep us from our call and we have only touched on a few of them, but I think the greatest is lack of commitment. I recall someone telling a woman of God that they wish they had her walk, and she said all it required was time with the Lord in prayer and study on a daily basis.

You have to put God first, period. If that sounds legalistic, then it is. If you want to do all that God has for you to do, you must put Him first in all things. I find myself at times getting side tracked from my studies and when I ask God what is wrong with me, this is what He shows me. These four things have to be the priority in your life:

Prayer
Study
Listen
Obey

Every morning before the rest of the house is up, or before you have to go to work or whatever you do in the morning, you must begin the day with God.

You do not have time not to. Your whole day is a mess without your time with the Lord. For those who have not done this before, I am challenging you to go one full week, spending the first hour of your day with the Lord.

You may ask, "An hour? That's too long", but I am telling you by the end of the week you will be saying, "Where did the time go? I'm not finished yet."

As I conclude part one of this epistle, I want to encourage you to take some time and meditate on what you have read. Do a little self-examination. Write down the blessings God has given to you: For instance life, health, home, food, and your family and of course, those no one knows about, but you. Remember all the times you know you were being watched over; the wrecks you avoided; the bank book that had more money in it than you knew about; the car repairs, the clothes, towels etc. that never seem to wear out, and all the other things God, in His great mercy, has done for you.

As you write them down, begin to thank Him for these things and let Him remind you that everything is a gift from Him and He wants you to give it away. Share your victories with other women. Encourage them about the goodness of God.

Remember, the Devil is a liar, we heard that over and over in Zambia... believe it!

God is calling, how are you going to respond?

Personal Notes

Part 2

Counting the Cost!

You know, sometimes you just do not want to do the work! You may be lazy, maybe you don't see any results of the ministry you have done; after all, you have been working at it for so long that you feel it's time to quit, to give up, but you cannot quit! Let us just count the cost, so we will not wear ourselves out or get discouraged.

Let me tell you a story about myself. When I was in school, as far back as I can remember I dreaded to hear my name called in class. I was deathly afraid; call it pride, but the truth was, I never felt smart enough. I grew up very poor. I had only a couple of dresses that my mom kept washed and ironed for me. The soles of my shoes flapped when I walked; that was somewhat neat though, because I would flap out a beat when I walked. I wore thick glasses, was very tall, sort of like Olive on Popeye. In addition to that, my dad was the neighborhood drunk who ran off with my girlfriend's mom and everyone knew it. These facts brought insecurity to me and I didn't like anyone looking at me.

The first time I married, I married a man much like my dad and went through some rough times. I remarried and that was not so good either. I found myself in a lock up ward after a suicide attempt and you think I would give my life to the Lord? Not me, I had it all together and besides, "they" told me to come to God. He would be like a father to me. Well, as you can see, my knowledge of a father was one who left you stranded when you needed him most, so my response was, "No thank you."

About a year after the suicide attempt when my second marriage was crumbling around me, I went to visit my in-laws and, out of respect, went to church with them. For the first time in my life, I heard the gospel message. I realized that my "prayers" were nothing more than requests, like that of a child writing a Christmas list. I saw for the first time in my life that I was a sinner and needed to repent to God and Him alone. I believed that Jesus died for my sins and that He really loved me. I was broken.

I made Him my Lord that Sunday, asking for forgiveness and receiving it. I experienced the weight of the world fall off my shoulders. Nothing changed, yet everything changed, and I have never looked back. He started healing a much-wounded woman from rejection, un-forgiveness, lack of self-worth, self-esteem and you name it. I found that when people asked me what was different about me, I had no problem talking about Jesus.

Women began inviting me to share with their Bible study and prayer groups. Before long, I started giving my testimony at many places. It was so easy, because I was talking about my best friend, the one who healed me and set me free.

The cost of ministry for me was time, was I willing to be available to go and do what God wanted me to? What will it cost you? You may be involved in something special to you, and it happens that one day you are called to be there for someone and it's on the day of your "special" thing...what do you do?

Luke 14:28-33
For which of you, intending to build a tower, does not sit down first and count the cost, whether he has enough to finish it - lest, after he has laid the foundation, and is not able to finish, all who see it begin to mock him, saying, 'This man began to build and was not able to finish.' Or what king, going to make war against another king, does not sit down first and consider whether he is able with ten thousand to meet him who comes against him with twenty thousand? Or else, while the other is still a great way off, he sends a delegation and asks conditions of peace. So likewise, whoever of you does not forsake all that he has cannot be My disciple.
NKJV

    What God wants us to know is this: The call on you and me is real. We are helping others by loving them into the kingdom of God and it is serious. The Lord will never give us more than we can handle. It is just that there will be times that ministry is inconvenient. Count the cost in your life whether it be time, lack of knowledge, money, family members, friends, or laziness. Or, you may not feel anointed. I want to be honest here, I've been there too.

    The fact that we are a living testimony or should be can be costly. It has happened to me on occasion, that if and when someone says or does something to a loved one, I react in an ungodly way and have been called on it. My life as a pastor's wife kept me in a fish bowl and was the exact training I needed and truthfully, sometimes I resented it, but I learned that was part of the cost for me. It kept me on my toes for the most part and when I fell, I always had Jesus to convict me, pick me up, and guide me to repentance first to Him and then to the person I offended. I don't like when this happens, but we all do it and Christ is always there to put things back in order.

I know people who have gotten up in the middle of the night to go help someone in the hospital. You may be asked to go to a foreign country, teach a Bible Study or many other things. You can do it. In Philippians 4, we are told the author says he has learned how to be content in every situation because he can do all things through Christ who strengthens him... that was one of the very first scriptures I memorized; it gave me comfort back then and it gives me courage now.

Whatever you think is too costly for you to give up, ask God for wisdom and a heart change if needed. He will work everything out for you when you have said yes in your heart to serve Him. You'll see.

Personal Notes

Part 3

Go for it!

Every time God opens a door for me to minister, I think, "Is this really you Lord?" I do not want to make a mistake. Does that sound familiar? I have heard people say, "I really need to pray about that," or "Let me pray about it" knowing they were stalling to keep from doing what they were supposed to do. What I want you to hear is this; pray about it and when you feel that nudge from God, be obedient. We all have to start some time.

The first time I went to Africa was with a team from our church in the year 2000. My husband announced that twelve people from the church were going to Zambia and I would be one of them. Well, oh great and mighty servant of the Lord that I was, said to the person sitting next to me, "God didn't tell me that: I'm not going." I had to repent from that, you can be sure. Within two weeks, we were in the county health clinic getting the first series of travel shots. God just worked it in me. Now I find myself doing whatever He puts in front of me to do. Maybe it is my age, but I want to do everything He allows me do for His kingdom. Whatever the reason, ministering is what keeps me alive.

Psalm 84:11
For the LORD God is a sun and shield; He gives grace and glory; no good thing does he withhold from those whose walk is blameless.

We have looked at some of the "whys" we are not fulfilling the call. We have looked at "counting the cost". What is left? Do you think God made a mistake? On the other hand, that you cannot do it? One time we adopted an old couple into our family by the name Mr. and Mrs. Jones. My children would say to Mrs. Jones, "But Jonesy, I can't", and she would tell them that cannot never could. That stayed with me all these years, it is such a simple statement with such great impact. If we will exclude the word can't/cannot, from our vocabulary, and remember the word of God that tells us we can do all things through Christ who strengthens us, we will not fail! God does not make mistakes; you truly are His vessel, His workmanship, His lump of clay. The master potter formed you.

Jeremiah 18:4
And the vessel that he made of clay was marred in the hand of the potter: so he made it again another vessel, as seemed good to the potter to make it.

In the commentaries, I gathered the following concept, that when the pot did not stand still in the working; it got out of shape; or some gravel or small stones having been incorporated with the mass of clay, made a breach causing the pot to be marred. Thus, the potter was obliged to knead up the clay again, place it on the wheel, and form it anew; it became a vessel that seemed good to the potter. The potter is the creator of his work, just like any artist or craftsman. If you have done any creative thing be it decorating, painting, crafts, etc., you have an understanding of this. I have done many projects in my life and understand completely how the creator has full ownership of what is being done and unlike God, I have thrown out my mistakes instead of re-working them. It's all a learning process in patience and grace.

Ezekiel 11:19
"I will take the stony heart out of their flesh"

God wants us to be gentle and loving. Things will come against you. Satan wants you to have hardness of heart and the sharp arrows and stones that the devil shoots at you through others can and will accomplish that. However, let us not forget that we have the armor of God with the shield of faith to protect our hearts. He has all the time in the world, but He has a ministry for you, a mission, and it is vital that you complete it. When given the opportunity, remember there are people to witness to and ministries that are in your heart to fulfill, that no one else can do. It is your call.

You are not a lost cause. If you do not conform to the potter's hands, and being God's minister, He will do what He has to do and re-form you into another pot, another vessel, smooth and beautiful. You are important to Him.

The breaking God does is causing you to become completely humbled and submitted, giving Him freedom to do even greater miracles through you. Some of us have never been broken… it really hurts when it happens, but submission to God is powerful. Moreover, when we are broken, we learn deep in our being that, truly, we are completely helpless without Him and that turns out to be the safest and most confident place you will ever want to be.

Once again, I want to take the opportunity to give some of my testimony about submission. Coming from the background I came from, submission to men was not a thing easily grasped by me. I loved the Lord with all my heart. I sang for Him and danced for Him. I ministered in His name and one day He brought me a wonderful Christian man to marry and "live happily ever after with", Not! I found out real quick that it was easy to let God be my husband, but a real person was not so easy. I love the Lord in my husband more that the man himself and that was and is a good thing, but when I became his wife, I learned he had many faults, not at all unlike myself.

I thought I was being a godly wife until one day in church a sister came up to me and said she had been praying for me and the Lord showed her I was not a submitted wife. I was so angry with her, but after a couple of days of stewing, I sat down with God and asked Him to show me. He led me to the scripture where we see the true submission that our Lord Jesus had; it was in the Garden of Gethsemane. I knew now that I had a huge problem. I went to my very dear sister and thanked her for loving me enough to tell me the truth about myself. You see that is what we should be about, helping each other reach our real potential in love.

We can ignore correction and God's word, but if we want to get anywhere in our walk with Him, and do what we know in our hearts, what He has called us to, we will ask Him to help us and He will.

Remember, you are God's vessel. What does that mean? Just what is a vessel? It is any kind of container or receptacle. The vessels of the Hebrew people were usually earthenware. Vessels made of glass, metal, leather, wicker, and stone were not uncommon either. These vessels were used to hold everything from documents to wine, fruits, and oil.

These words all mean "an implement or utensil" of any kind. When we become God's vessels we learn the importance of what it means to be a hollow utensil. As hollow and empty vessels allow God to put whatever He wants in it.

VESSEL
In a broader sense, ships are sometimes referred to as vessels since they are the receptacles of people. In an even broader sense, vessel refers to people who carry within them the knowledge of God just as any clay vessel reflects the craftsmanship of its potter, so people reflect the craftsmanship of God. Man is in accordance with His plan (Rom 9:21-23).
(from Nelson's Illustrated Bible Dictionary, Copyright © 1986, Thomas Nelson Publishers)

VESSEL
**The word "vessel" has passed into Christian theology as signifying simply a human being.
(International Standard Bible Encyclopedia, Electronic Database Copyright 1996 by Biblesoft)**

Do you recall when we talked about how Christ asked Saul/Paul in the book of Acts, "Why do you kick against the pricks?" Paul was not holding still on the potter's wheel, and if there was hope for Paul to avoid being broken, what about us? Ultimately, Paul was reformed in the hands of the potter and went on to be one of the most powerful Christians in history.

Just as Paul was; around 60 AD; understand that God wants to do something in us. Our God has made each one of us into a specialized vessel to fill. Then we are used when, where and how He wants to use us... Do you understand this? Do you know how important you are?

Just think how hard it was for Paul: Paul a man who had not seen Christ, yet he was prepared in so many ways to minister. What he did not know, he learned shortly after his conversion. God taught him using the mistakes he made; therefore, they became Paul's teaching tools.

How many of us have been bad and out of the will of God? Yet everything you have ever done or gone through can be a valuable tool. As an example, when you are ministering. I always tell people I am ministering to, that my testimonies and experiences are mine; it is the word of God that is the life changer. I then show them how God's word worked for me and in me. The Bible is our instruction manual for life. Also, Jesus never gives us more to do than we can handle. Remember, He sent us a helper.

John 16:29-33
Jesus' disciples said, "Now you are speaking clearly and without figures of speech. Now we can see that you know all things and that you do not even need to have anyone ask you questions. This makes us believe that you came from God." "You believe at last!" Jesus answered. "But a time is coming, and has come, when you will be scattered, each to his own home. You will leave me all alone. Yet I am not alone, for my Father is with me. "I have told you these things, so that in me you may have peace. In this world you will have trouble. But take heart! I have overcome the world."

In speaking to His Father, Jesus says:

John 17:6
"I have revealed you to those whom you gave me out of the world. They were yours; you gave them to me and they have obeyed your word. Now they know that everything you have given me comes from you. For I gave them the words you gave me and they accepted them. They knew with certainty that I came from you, and they believed that you sent me. I pray for them. I am not praying for the world, but for those you have given me, for they are yours."

This was a prayer time just for the disciples, not the lost. There is a time to pray only for the followers of Christ. Are they special? You bet they are. Are you special? The answer is yes, a resounding yes!

Of course, Jesus prayed for the lost as well, just as He wants you too, but this prayer was specifically for the ones who were going to minister His gospel. That is you and me. We get special prayers; I just know it.

John 17:10-19
"All I have is yours, and all you have is mine. And glory has come to me through them. I will remain in the world no longer, but they are still in the world, and I am coming to you. Holy Father, protect them by the power of your name-the name you gave me-so that they may be one as we are one. While I was with them, I protected them and kept them safe by that name you gave me. None has been lost except the one doomed to destruction so that Scripture would be fulfilled. "I am coming to you now, but I say these things while

I am still in the world, so that they may have the full measure of my joy within them. I have given them your word and the world has hated them, for they are not of the world any more than I am of the world. My prayer is not that you take them out of the world but that you protect them from the evil one. They are not of the world, even as I am not of it. Sanctify them by the truth; your word is truth. As you sent me into the world, I have sent them into the world. For them I sanctify myself, that they too may be truly sanctified."

I remember hearing that I could not be in ministry because I had been married before. I struggled even after a conversation about this with my pastor. Then one morning while I was on my patio having my quiet time with the Lord, I read this scripture.

1 Corinthians 6:9-11
Do you not know that the wicked will not inherit the kingdom of God? Do not be deceived: Neither the sexually immoral nor idolaters nor adulterers nor male prostitutes nor homosexual offenders nor thieves nor the greedy nor drunkards nor slanderers nor swindlers will inherit the kingdom of God. And that is what some of you were. But you were washed, you were sanctified, you were justified in the name of the Lord Jesus Christ and by the Spirit of our God.

That is we, new creations in Christ. Everything we did before we made Jesus our Lord, everything we did before we were born again, is under the blood of Jesus. Hallelujah, that is worth shouting about. If that were all we preached, it would be a great sermon.

The word goes on to teach us about our lives as we are doing good, doing the will of God.

1Peter 3:13-22
Who is going to harm you if you are eager to do good? But even if you should suffer for what is right, you are blessed. "Do not fear what they fear; do not be frightened." But in your hearts set apart Christ as Lord. Always be prepared to give an answer to everyone who asks you to give the reason for the hope that you have. But do this with gentleness and respect, keeping a clear conscience, so that those who speak maliciously against your good behavior in Christ may be ashamed of their slander. It is better, if it is God's will, to suffer for doing good than for doing evil. For Christ died for sins once for all, the righteous for the unrighteous, to bring you to God. He was put to death in the body but made alive by the Spirit, through whom also he went and preached to the spirits in prison who disobeyed long ago when God waited patiently in the days of Noah while the ark was being built. In it only a few people, eight in all, were saved through water, and this water symbolizes baptism that now saves you also-not the removal of dirt from the body but the pledge of a good conscience toward God. It saves you by the resurrection of Jesus Christ, who has gone into heaven and is at God's right hand-with angels, authorities and powers in submission to him.

Paul had some powerful words for Timothy in both books, but we will focus on 2 Timothy 1, as we see Paul give charge to Timothy, we should read it as though Paul is speaking to us.

2 Timothy 1:1-11
Paul, an apostle of Christ Jesus by the will of God, according to the promise of life that is in Christ Jesus, To Timothy, my dear son: Grace, mercy and peace from God the Father and Christ Jesus our Lord. I thank God, whom I serve, as my forefathers did, with a clear conscience, as night and day I constantly remember you Recalling your tears, I long to see you, so that I may be filled with joy. I have been reminded of your sincere faith, which first lived in your grandmother Lois and in your mother Eunice and, I am persuaded, now lives in you also. For this reason, I remind you to fan into flame the gift of God, which is in you through the laying on of my hands. For God did not give us a spirit of timidity, but a spirit of power, of love and of self-discipline. So do not be ashamed to testify about our Lord, or ashamed of me his prisoner. But join with me in suffering for the gospel, by the power of God, who has saved us and called us to a holy life-not because of anything we have done but because of his own purpose and grace. This grace was given us in Christ Jesus before the beginning of time, but it has now been revealed through the appearing of our Savior, Christ Jesus, who has destroyed death and has brought life and immortality to light through the gospel. And of this gospel I was appointed a herald and an apostle and a teacher

Paul continues to instruct them.

2 Timothy 2:1-14
You then, my son, be strong in the grace that is in Christ Jesus. And the things you have heard me

say in the presence of many witnesses entrust to reliable men who will also be qualified to teach others. Endure hardship with us like a good soldier of Christ Jesus. No one serving as a soldier gets involved in civilian affairs-he wants to please his commanding officer. Similarly, if anyone competes as an athlete, he does not receive the victor's crown unless he competes according to the rules. The hardworking farmer should be the first to receive a share of the crops. Reflect on what I am saying, for the Lord will give you insight into all this. Remember Jesus Christ, raised from the dead, descended from David. This is my gospel, for which I am suffering even to the point of being chained like a criminal. But God's word is not chained. Therefore I endure everything for the sake of the elect, that they too may obtain the salvation that is in Christ Jesus, with eternal glory. Here is a trustworthy saying: If we died with him, we will also live with him; if we endure, we will also reign with him. If we disown him, he will also disown us; if we are faithless, he will remain faithful, for he cannot disown himself. What you heard from me, keep as the pattern of sound teaching, with faith and love in Christ Jesus. Guard the good deposit that was entrusted to you-guard it with the help of the Holy Spirit who lives in us.

How much easier could our instructions be? We are soldiers in God's army, keeping our minds on the ministry and calling. God has entrusted you with His word and anointing and expects you to use it. Remember, you are the vessel created by the potter's hands for His purpose.

2 Timothy 2:20-21

In a large house there are articles not only of gold and silver, but also of wood and clay; some are for noble purposes and some for ignoble. If a man cleanses himself from the latter, he will be an instrument for noble purposes, made holy, useful to the Master and prepared to do any good work.

The Master designed you for a noble purpose. At some point in my walk with God, I heard a teaching about the difference in the vessels the potter makes. The teaching was comparing a Ming Vase with a clay pot. The Ming Vase is a thing of beauty having little practical value that we look at and admire on occasion. On the other hand, we use the clay pot repeatedly, even when it becomes chipped or cracked. It is imperative that you know you do not have to be perfect to be effective. I am a perfect example of that. Besides, anytime we think we have it all together, well that is when we are in real trouble. The only way to minister is with humility and love, cracks, chips and all. Totally depending on God, not self.

One time on my way home from a speaking engagement, I was given a first class seat. Well, I thought I was something, I didn't have to wait in a long line, I had it all! Then along came reality, I stepped on my pants leg and ripped the hem. As I walked down the airport dragging my pant leg behind me I had my reality check and repented thanking God for the experience; both the good and bad of it. I purchased band aides, went in the bathroom and taped my pants leg up. Whenever I start to think, "I'm all that" [and everyone does on occasion] I think about that trip.

2 Timothy 1:6-7

For this reason, I remind you to fan into flame the gift of God, which is in you through the laying on of my hands. For God did not give us a spirit of timidity, but a spirit of power, of love and of self-discipline.

When you stand up to minister, remember that Satan wants you to think you cannot do it. He will try to put fear in you, but as you can see, God did not give that spirit to you. He gave you love and self-control. Satan will bring up your past; let him, you are forgiven and your past is what you have been set free from. Remember in Revelation we are reminded that we overcome by the Blood of the Lamb and the word of our testimony - that is powerful. Jesus took your past sins; He now owns them. Hallelujah!

Romans 16:19-20
Everyone has heard about your obedience, so I am full of joy over you; but I want you to be wise about what is good, and innocent about what is evil. The God of peace will soon crush Satan under your feet. The grace of our Lord Jesus be with you.

Your responsibility is to keep the gifts stirred. Use them with all wisdom, the wisdom that God has given to you. The more you use the gifts, the more gifts you will receive and the more comfortable you will be with them.

My spiritual mother told me a story that went like this. If someone gives you a beautiful scarf, but you never wear it or use it, will that person ever want to give you anything else? *What good is a beautiful gift if you keep it in the box or in a drawer?* Use the gifts God gives you. He has much more for you.

Continue stirring up the gift. What are you doing with the gift/gifts that you have received? Have you laid them down? Do you know what they are? Have you ever used them to the full potential God wants you too?

Let us refresh ourselves. Do you have a ministry? Have you laid it down? Do you want it back? Do you know what it is?

Listen to this scripture, this is a familiar scene.

John 21:1-3
Afterward Jesus appeared again to his disciples, by the Sea of Tiberias. It happened this way: [the 7th. Appearance after His death] Simon Peter, Thomas (called Didymus), Nathanael from Cana in Galilee, the sons of Zebedee, and two other disciples were together. "I'm going out to fish," Simon Peter told them, and they said, "We'll go with you." So they went out and got into the boat, but that night they caught nothing.

None of the commentaries quit agree with why they were fishing. Some say they went back to their old jobs. Some say they were idle; some say they were just hanging around together. This is exactly how easy it is to see what scripture means in Mark 14. That scripture tells us, when the shepherd of the sheep has been stricken, the sheep will scatter. Who knows? Nevertheless, one thing is for sure; they went back to fishing for fish!

John 21:4-15

Early in the morning, Jesus stood on the shore, but the disciples did not realize that it was Jesus. He called out to them, "Friends, haven't you any fish?" "No," they answered. He said, "Throw your net on the right side of the boat and you will find some." When they did, they were unable to haul the net in because of the large number of fish. Then the disciple whom Jesus loved said to Peter, "It is the Lord!" As soon as Simon Peter heard him say, "It is the Lord," he wrapped his outer garment around him (for he had taken it off) and jumped into the water. The other disciples followed in the boat, towing the net full of fish, for they were not far from shore, about a hundred yards. When they landed, they saw a fire of burning coals there with fish on it, and some bread. Jesus said to them, "Bring some of the fish you have just caught." Simon Peter climbed aboard and dragged the net ashore. It was full of large fish, 153, but even with so many the net was not torn. Jesus said to them, "Come and have breakfast." None of the disciples dared ask him, "Who are you?" They knew it was the Lord. Jesus came, took the bread and gave it to them, and did the same with the fish. This was now the third time Jesus appeared to his disciples after he was raised from the dead. When they had finished eating, Jesus said to Simon Peter, [Peter had said how much more he loved Christ than all the others, do you remember? And it seems like Jesus is giving him an opportunity to redeem himself...maybe.] "Simon son of John, do you truly love me more than these?" "Yes, Lord," he said, "you know that I love you." Jesus said, "Feed my lambs."

The babes, the young, tender, eager, unlearned, hurt, hungry, easily destroyed, and many other things, but they are all infants. Jesus said to bring the little ones to Him. The babies need the most care of all. Just like a newborn baby in the natural world require full time care, so do the ones in the spiritual world. Our ministry is to train them, feed them and encourage them to grab a hold of Jesus' hand and walk. To go from the milk of the Word to the meat of God's word so they are able to stand in every situation.

We all are ahead of someone. We all have something to give away. That is exciting to me and should be to you as well.

John 21:16
Again Jesus said, "Simon son of John, do you truly love me?" He answered, "Yes, Lord, you know that I love you." Jesus said, "Take care of my sheep."

The original text once again says, **"feed my sheep"**. I looked up the meaning in the commentaries and the word feed in this verse meant to tend, as a shepherd would a flock. That means much more than feed. It means to do all the things a more mature sheep would need done for it.

John 21:17
The third time he said to him, "Simon son of John, do you love me?" Peter was hurt because Jesus asked him the third time, "Do you love me?" He said, "Lord, you know all things; you know that I love you." Jesus said, "Feed my sheep.

This time the word feed simply means to feed. What Jesus was saying now is to continue to feed the mature with mature food. Do not stop taking care of God's flock!

John 21:18-19
I tell you the truth, when you were younger you dressed yourself and went where you wanted; but when you are old you will stretch out your hands, and someone else will dress you and lead you where you do not want to go." Jesus said this to indicate the kind of death by which Peter would glorify God. Then he said to him, "Follow me!"

Once again, Jesus is saying to us "Come, follow me, I will make you fishers of men, women, and children, come! There is nothing more exciting and fulfilling than when you lead someone to Christ, or when you pray for someone and the power of God touches that person. These are the most rewarding times of your life.

One of my favorite scriptures of all time; and I have many, is in Jeremiah.

Jeremiah 29:11
For I know the thoughts that I think toward you, says the LORD, thoughts of peace and not of evil, to give you a future and a hope. NKJV

The Lord is telling us that He thinks about us. He is planning things for us to do. He wants us to walk in the plan and know that it is a plan full of peace with a future full of hope. This scripture is evidence that the Master of all things ordained your ministry. All you need to do is, do it! God orders the steps of the righteous. Do not look to the right or left, but walk the straight path He has laid before you.

The question is, have you been called? Of course you have! Are you ready to have the flame bellowed? Are you ready to allow God to put more fuel on the fire? Do you want to fulfill all God has for you? Remember, you are not alone, He is right there with you. Whatever your ministry is, whether it is being a mom, a rich person, a poor person, a wife, an evangelist, a missionary, a children's worker, a teacher, a prayer warrior, or an encourager, whatever it is, God is in it with you.

He said to the disciples, "**Come follow me**". They laid down their nets and followed Him. To you He is saying the same thing, "Will you follow"?

Now is the time to make out your list, pray for direction, and pray daily. Then comes the hard part; wait for the doors to open and open they will. God is looking for those who will trust and obey.

Congratulations, you are officially on your way!

Personal Notes

About the Author

Mary Murray is an evangelist, missionary, author and speaker. She has been in the ministry for over 30 years, preaching, leading worship, retreats, Bible studies, and various other ministries both nationally and internationally which ultimately led to starting Mission Ministries.

Her personal testimony is of one tragedy turned triumph; once having tried to commit suicide, she has come from a state of rejection and torment to an exciting life in Jesus

Her heart's desire is for women to be set free and God's Word to become real in their lives; that they grow in the knowledge and understanding of who they are in the Lord. Her teaching is not a "Head Knowledge" but a "Heart Knowledge" because of what God has walked her through.

To contact Mary for your next retreat or gathering go to:
mary@missionm.org
314-769-7129 Visit us on the web @: www.missionm.org

Made in the USA
Las Vegas, NV
28 February 2024